BLACKOUT AND POETRY

BLACKOUT AND POETRY

MARION ROBINSON

ARPress
ILLUMINATING IDEAS
EMPOWERING VOICES

ARPress LLC
45 Dan Road Suite 5
Canton MA 02021
Hotline: 1(888) 821-0229
Fax: 1(508) 545-7580

Ordering Information:
Quantity sales. Special discounts are available on quantity purchases by corporations, associations, and others. For details, contact the publisher at the address above.

Printed in the United States of America.

ISBN-13:	Softcover	979-8-89330-847-1
	eBook	979-8-89330-848-8

Library of Congress Control Number: 2024901832

CONTENTS

INTRODUTION

Thank you to my sister Dr. Marguerite Coke Maxwell. My Mother Martha Jane Robinson Coke, my Brother's Rookie Renaldo Coke. William James Coke. Each one was a part of my life. It was my Sister that gave me the inspiration to write this book. My family helped me. But it took me some time to begin. My name is Marion Robinson. I use to Live in N.Y.C most of my life. It's hard to write what I can remember about part of my live. I'm hoping what I may say or express in my writing I just may help someone. I had many Jobs from the Horn & Hordes, Hospitals, a Bank, but the best job was with the Rail Road. Thank you all that was and is Part of my life. Also to Mrs. Andrea Carr I say thank you for being there for me and giving me words of wisdom.

The backdrop here is a sixty eight years old black man, looking back over my life. My name is Marion Robinson.

Thinking about where can I start? My story may be able to help someone that is on the road of Destruction. Can a detour take place? Yes? It happens to me. Some may say this could not happen to me. Let me tell you it can. You see in my younger days I loved to party. I had no cares in the world.my get away was New York City, and Philadelphia .between the two cities was my playing ground. I was born in New York City in Harlem Hospital in 1943.living on 133 street, and Hell's Kitchen. I could say was not the best, but I had more than the other kids had. Within my own family had a difficult time coming up in life ,not knowing I had any siblings this was a big blow to me in my life. That is another story that one day will be told, l at a another time. Let's get back to the story; I was going to school for electrics I graduated, the school got me a job working for the rail road. In New York City. (the Big Apple)this was in 1973. I had no seniority just like so many that came before me I had to work my way up the ladder. The door has been open for blacks. There were some good times we had people from different walks of life worked on the rail road. We became a family.

Some of the foremen's was doing their own thing. And some of them were pissed off because hiring of the blacks at that time; there was not even a hand full of black foreman's most of the foremen were white and had their own family members working for the rail road. This was part of the norm and part of life.

Decimation was there, and it had to come to an end. It was hard for blacks, we had to be at our best, and walk the line. One day something begin to happen as we were waiting for our orders from head quarter; In the locker room where we all mat, there were different men working in different departments, from third.

Rail men, to track men, class A,B operator then come the small machine operator, all in the same locker room. It was full of men. From the senior men to the younger men. Some were getting dressed, others playing cards, and some were eating. The door opened and walked in someone we never seen before. A big black man walked in he looked around, he had a little smile on his face. And in his hand he had a piece of paper with names written on it. He stood about 5'8 dark skin about 210 pounds he had a round face. He opened his mouth and said my name is (Mr. West) when I call your name out stand on the right side of the locker room.

I found myself on the right side of the room. Forty men in all. He said am your new foreman, some of you may get to like me, or hate me. Now here are my rules; if you are late, I will send you home, don't let me catch you drinking on the job. I don't care after you are off work. You are here to do a job. And I expect you to do the job. There will be over time. And for you knew comers you need to wait your turn for the over time. seniority comes first. We looked one another, one of the senior men said O shit! I know this nut! He's a ball buster.(West.) said if you keep your nose clean you will have a job if you listen to what I tell you. You will go a long way,. you new men put in for bid when they come out. This is how you can move up the ladder, hear what I tell you I don't wont' to see none of you miss up. Some will be foreman others will be class 1 or class 2 operators, others will move on within the company. Now this leads me into my story I worked for (Mr. West) for about (2 to 3) years Yes he was hard but he was fare. Each time a bid came out I put in for it, I walked in one hot morning, Mr. West came up to me , I said to myself what have I done? As he walk up to me with nothing on his face. I got the name New York .He called out too me (New York) You got the bid in Hudson, NY as a class two operator. I did! Yes you did.

The next thing I asked where is Hudson, NY? Look on your time table. This was a day of rejoicing for me. Some of my co-works got bid also some in NY, others in conn. I was the only one that came from NYC. I was feeling good all that day, knowing I will no longer will be under (Mr. West) I could not wait to Get home to tell my family, I lived next door to my mother in the next building .I was hopefully they would be happy for me. Me being the oldest of my sables.

I had no car at that time. Could not drive, the only transportation I know was the bus, and train. I got home seeing my mother, I told her the good news, She looked at me her face had no expression on it. I had to get to Hudson by the next week, to cover my job. My mother said what are you going to do in Hudson, NY? You don't know anyone there, where are you going to stay when you get there? Are you going to move to Hudson? If I like it I may. My brother Rookie next to me said If you do move this will gave me a place to come. Man get out of my face, do your thing! And my sister Penny said do your own thing bro you got my blessing. This maybe the best thing for you. You know what you need to do She was married at this time and not living at home. The week end was coming up I packed my work close and dress closes The rail road gave each employee work pass this pass got us to and from work. The week end came I got on the train at that time it was called the Pennsylvania rail road. I left early in the morning about 5 or 6 am the ride seemed to be a long ride on the train had what is called a deadhead car. For employees this time I did not ride it, this time I was a passenger. I had my bags with me. I got off in Hudson NY and o man! I looked around. the train station looked like the ones you would see in a cow boy movie. but it looked up dated. I took a cab and went to a hotel .I checked in for the week and made arraignment for the following week I don't get paid for two more weeks. The management worked along with me.

My food was included with my bill. This was a blessing for me. I walked out of the Holtal as I looked around on the Main St . I did not see any beer can in the street, nor any papers in the streets, I said to myself man this is a clean city. As I walked down the street I met some of my co-works some of them was cool, other were cold as ice. I seen a church on the Main street. Not knowing this will become my home church. I stayed in Hudson that week. Monday I went to cover my new job. I got to know some of the men that wound be in my group, and my new foreman. A red faced man about 195 pounds and about 5'7, he had a big belly.

He loved his beer also, Now you see for yourself were am going, I had to get all my things from NYC to Hudson, NY. A man I worked with came to me said I know a place on Columbian street, I will take you there after work. It's a two bed room apartment. You will like it. Great! I became good friends with John. He looked out for me; He had a moving truck when you are ready I will move you from NY to Hudson, How much will you charge me O I will say about $250.00 I said ok.

After work he took me to this three story house, across the street was a junk yard this junk yard was for used cars. He ringed the bell. We went in and went up three floors, a short woman open the door.is this the young man you told me about, this is him. She ask me where do you live now? I said right now am staying at the Hotel here in Hudson, I need to find an apartment to live. Where are you from? Am from N.Y.C O! You're from N ..YC. Yes mam she looked at me with a smile ok let's look at the apt. we walked down the stairs to the next floor. She open the door, and as she open the door the first thing that came out of my mouth was Yes! Yes! yes! Think you Lord. The rent is 450.00 per month can you pay it. Yes I can. She did not ask me for any security She seized me and caught me off guide. Did you go to church Sunday, I said yes I did .You must be that young man with that beautiful voice. This Sunday I did go to church. I heard about you from some of the members at Church.What do you think about my church? I like it.

Am thinking about joying it. When I lived in North Philadelphia, I was raised as an melodist in AM.E church I became one of the Sunday school teacher; at an early age. Mrs. Carr was a Baptist Church. And I loved what I heard when I was there. I was a church goer all of my life. I had to, this was the way I was brought up. I made mistakes in my life also But I put my trust in God. There have been times I was down and out, and I could not see my way out in different cases, it was God that stepped in not man, you see he opened the doors for me. Some of my down falls was on me and others was not. Mrs. Carr was a short woman about 5'6 Mr. Roberts about 5'7 I moved to Hudson that Saterday I did Joyed (MR. Roberts MRS Carr). Church that Sunday I became a Baptist.

I lived in Hudson for about 10 years, am cutting short some of the story to get to the main points In Hudson you needed a car, for shopping, going from town, to town. The only main transporting was the bus, or the rail road. I move from NYC, to Hudson into my new apt. I'll call her (Mr. Roberts) & (Mrs. Carr) she became my second mother an Mr. roberts my second father. Both of became my family.

I got a car before I known how to drive my first car was a ford white about 1963or1965 it had power windows. My down payment was only $1.00 believe it or not all together I paid $550.00 for this car. The car dealer made all the arguments the car ins. Got me the car tags.you see each week I would go by to see what the deal ship had for sail, one day I stop in and I looked in the back I seen this white ford setting, it seemed as if it was calling out to me. I asked the dealer what about that white ford that is setting in the back. It has not move sends I've been coming here. can I hear it run? And test drive it, the dealer took me for a test drive believe or not, I only need something to get me to and from work. O I see I believe you are looking for a new car. He began to take down my information. I told the dealer I will not pick the car up until it is all paid for. And I did just that I had some of my co-works drive me to and from work.my mine was made up I got to learn how to drive.

In about four year I had to get a car not knowing how drive, I talk driving lessons I tried three, to four times to pass the driving test. Five times I tried to pass the driving test I pass on the last test; in my own car. Now it was up to me and me alone to get on the high way and to learn the short cuts from town to town.

(MR.C & Mr.R) were over joyed for me. Mrs.C said, to me now you can see your family by driving to NYC, It took me some time to drive from Hudson too NYC, I got lost many time even today I still do.I drove to my mothers, man she was over joyed seeing me, she call ever one in the family.and her friends.

I could not say no, I was letting people drive my car. My mother jumped all over me.

Man what's wrong with you letting people drive your car, If something happens to the car, or the person or persons in the car you will be reposable. The only thing I could say your right. Stop!!! letting people drive your car, you hear me, My mother could not drive; but she now the right and wrongs about driving.

My brother next to me, looked at me He said Man you are sick letting people driving your car, I can't drive will you let me drive your car as well? YES or NO.

I said No. you need a driver's license, you and mom is jumping all over me get off my back; both of you are right I'll stop OK! You all win. My mine was racing thinking about what was said. Knowing they are right. Driving back to Hudson that's when I made up my mine. I will stop letting others drive my car. some of my co-worker asked me can I use your car, to do my shopping, or can I use your car to go to the next town? And this became a long term I had to say no! Saying no was hard for me at one point. But I did do it. Soon they stopped asking to drive my car. Hudson is a smile town, with bars, church's barber shops, shopping malls on the out shirts of town, a Hospital that sets on a hill. In town you had small little shops up and down the main street. also you had the after hour jots Two brother ran it. This was were most of the rail road works would go , after work, Yes I did to. but I would go on Friday night after work.You could walk up and down the main street in comford. The community itself looked fined, but it to too had a bad side as well, on the job, in the bars, but we learn how to deal with it. Most of the young people moved away, we had two, three ,or four, main business or company in Hudson, NY.

The rail road was one of the main incomes for Hudson. Most of the men worked for the rail road. Some of them had more time than I had. But I was making more money than thy were. I was a class Two operator. Putting money away I did not do. I loved to party on Friday nights I would go out to the bars, you see I loved my beer, and Rum and Coke. These was my drinks. Nothing came to mine about putting money away for a raining day. Time passed one Friday night being home, I got tired of being in Hudson, I got into my car and I drove to Albany, NY I got to know my way around in Albany, like I said I loved to party. I did in N.Y.C I gusts my mother was happy I moved to Hudson She new How I was, I loved to drink. My sister I know she was happy I moved as well, she must have jump for joy when I move. I can hear her say, Lord thank you for getting my brother out of N.Y.C thank you, thank you, keep my brother in your care. I droved to Albany I park my car. I went to bar to bar, in one area from a Gay bar, strait bars, some of the bars were mixed. I got alone with Gay people they became friends of mine. I never put any one down, even to this day; I am the same way today. I don't care if you are Black, or white. We all must got along with each other, no matter your way of life, or your outlook of life. If anything we do harm to each other by not helping one another or caring for one another. This is our down fall in life.

I got to know some of the people. Some became friends of mine set me up Jo, give the hold bar a drinks on me. Their maybe about six people in the bar when I did that. Most of the bar tender got to know me. And I got to know them as well. On this night I jump from bar to the next. I was feeling no pain; drinks was coming to me, I believed my mojo was working. I got into my car; drove about fifteen blocks from where I was. This time I was in a night club. Music playing, people dancing, glasses being filed; I felt no pain. Not knowing I was killing myself; by doing this crazy thing. I be gain not to remember the things I did and sided, my brain begin to shut down. Even thrown I can see and hear what was going on around me. But I became a walking zombie.

The question is did I become addicted to boozes? Yes I did, unknown to me. I became an alcoholic; no one could tell me anything; I only drink over the weekend; that was my down fall, an alcoholic is a person may drink doing the week or weekends you are an alcoholic, you let alcohol take control of you. You become depended on alcohol .alcohol can take over your actions, the way you think, what you say to family members and siblings, thank about it, when you are drinking, you don't remember what comes out of your mouth. people may come up to you, do you remember what you said or did last night. Most likely you do not. You just had a blackout, you are in a coma.it can be short term, or even long term.the more you drink the deeper you get. It was about three o clock on Saturday morning. I stared up the car, thinking I was ok to drive back to Hudson. I had about thirty to thirty three miles to drive, the roads had hills, sharp caves, detours, and small towns. The police was out in these small towns also. looking for speeder and drink drivers.

If you had ask me are you drink I would have said Hell No! I had two ways to coming back from Albany, taking (9- W or 9-J) I don't remember. The only thing I do remember getting into the car driving off down the Street, Now I had to go up ramps, take the thruway 1-87 toward NY/Mass turnpike. I had to Paid totals. Until this day I don't understand how did I get from point A-to point B, I have heard many people say I don't remember doing this or that, and you say to yourself why can't you remember? I have going to Albany for some time. In the back of my mine I must have stored a road map in the back of my mine; and filed it away in my mine, you may have said I can do it with my eyes closed. Or I can drive to point A-B with my eyes closed. Just think about that for one moment; can you? the mine is a tricky thing. Even if you're not drinking. You become marred in your thanking. I had to go though small towns , like East Greenbush.N.Y Castleton on Hudson N.Y Coerymans,N.Y NewBalmore,N.Y Stuyvesant,N.Y Coxsackie,N.Y Stockport,N.Y Stormvillie,N.Y. there could be more little town I may have left out, or missed. What came to my mine, why didn't the police or the state police stop me? If I had gone though the total booth and paid my money they could have stopped me as well. None of the above happed. I don't remember what happed between Albany and on the out shirts of Hudson, N.Y I was coming out of my

sleeper, I heard sirens going off behind me, red lights flashing, I pull over to the side of the road, two police offices got out their police car, walked towards my car. One on one side the other on the other. One had a flash light, the one that had the flash light shined it in to my car, the police officer came up on the driver side, tap on my window I rolled down my window, I turn off the radio.

The officer that was on my side said; do you knows why we stop you? I said no sir. Well you were bobbing in and out on the road. Where are you coming from? Albany Sir. Have you been drinking? I said O Shit what have I done? Then it hit me! How in the world did I get from Albany? To outside of Hudson just about fifteen blocks from home. So close yet so far. My mine seem to come back into focus, I said to the officer thank you for stopping me, get out the car sir. Yes sir I said. Then he asked me to walk a straight line, I tried to walk it, but I was going one side to the other, the time must have been 5am in the morning the sun was just about to come up. On the spot they gave me a breath test it came out to be 1.8 I was taken off to jail; my car was impounded. I was in county jail over the week end in Hudson; just three blocks from home. In jail some were in jail for fighting, being disorderly, some in for being to tipsy, most of the men would be out that Monday, I had to go to court that Monday morning I had one phone call. I called Mrs. Carr my land lord, She said ok we will see you when you come home, this was the first time I was in jail for driving under the influence of alcohol. The day came when I had to go to court. The court appointed to me a legal aid I could not afford a lawyer, the lawyer said to me you don't have a leg to stand on, your breath lever was 1.8 that not good how do you what to pled, I told him well sir. I was in the wrong! And I thank God I did not kill some or myself, I stood up in court of the judge the judge asked me how do you pled? Guilty sir. My Lawyer pled my case, I don't remember what judge I had I would call Judge Bing. Your Honor sir, My client don't not have any criminal record, He's working for the rail road for four years now, he's an outstanding cities.

Made an miss, I do believe it will not happen again, sir. This was an eye opener for him, Mr. Robinson have seen for himself what he have done was wrong, drinking and driving dose not mix, The judge said Mr. Robinson you stand before me, I do hope I will not see you in my court any more, from this day forward have you learned what kind of trouble you are in yes sir. I will accept your pled, I fine you guilty thirty days in jail and $1,500.00 find. If you don't have it, you can make argument thought the court clerk, to pay the find. Mr. Robinson you may go to work, but you must report to county jail after work. And you can not work over the week end Do I make myself care. Yes sir also you must report to AA after your time is served. This is a must you got that Mr. Robinson yes sir. And your license is suspended for one year. This was a kicker in the head, I made arraignments with the court to pay $50.00 per month. You don't think when your license is taken away what that will mean; it's a privilege to drive a car. It's not a right. Too many have forgotten that. Today looking at the youth of today; To many are drinking, taking drugs, smoking weed. And get behind the wheel of a car, what happens they end up killing themselves loved one or family member, or anyone that is in the way. That becomes a troubling the thing. I to being a young man at the time, drugs, was never part of my life. Boozes, and beer was. Let's party that what came to my mine over the weekends. What I did than, the youth are doing it today. But today it's more troublesome, some are going to school tipsy after a night of drinking.

That morning I went back to jail, it was launch time, I don't remember what we had. The jail was cleaned out just about two or three men were there. In my sell I begin to think what am I going to do? What am I going to tell my family? Will I still l have my apartment? when am out of jail. Will I still have my job? How will I get my car out of the car pound? question On top of question? That's what I had. I said to myself I'll deal with all this when I get out. I did what I did now I have to pay for it. Shit I was a big numskull, a thickheaded. Time was going to be fast. Before I known it ; It was time for me to go to work, they let me out. I had to be at work at 8am they let me go about 7.30am I walk down Warren Street, down to Front Street, to the train station this was the place that we all met. People were going to work, getting their tickets for the month at the ticket booth, some passages going to N.Y.C for work. Others getting off at different stops. Most of the passage you see each day. Going to work. This was a everyday thing. There are trucks, van's, cars, that had the name of the railroad.

Parked outside of the train station. The name at one time was The Pennsylvania Rail road than the name changed to Metro North Rail Road. When they took over, some said it would be better for the rail road. Things did change. Tracks were repaired. Old ties replaced with new ones. From Albany to N.Y.C my gain got into the van and we went to work, replacing old ties, I had what was called tire destroyer, I had to put the old ties into this machine grine them up, the chips would fall into a hoper. This was one of the first machine we had gotten. It didn't work all that wall.

This machine was very dirty. You now have a little look into what I did for the railroad. My job did get better in the future, the days went by kind of fast, for me to get out jail. I was kind of surprise, no one ask me anything about what happen to me over the weekends, or why am not driving my car any more. I can understand why people drive their cars without a driving license. Today do I condone it, no I don't. I did the same thing. Sometimes it comes from not understanding the law; but also it can come from ignorance of the law. Doing your own thing. The day came when I was released, and could go back home for good. I went home,took a hot bath but something happened to me I looked into the mirror I saw my reflection in it, I looked deep down within myself with conviction, I said to myself; what's wrong with you. Get yourself together, and pull yourself together, and stop this mass. On that day my life changed for the better.one thing I must say I could not have done this on my own. I had to have a higher hope, for me it Jesus Christ, but for other it maybe Jehovah, Rabbi.

I don't care what you call your higher power, you need one you can not do it by yourself. Think about it, you must seek deep down within yourself and levied it to your higher power, but the help must come from you.one can not blame others for their mistakes in life. We all have a cross to bear, and we do need help from others. But most of us don't wish to say so. I had to look within myself. Looking deep within me, helped me to go to my AA (Alcoholics Annonymous) meetings and to share my experience's. Others did the same thing, mothers against drink drivers was just beginning, and in class was their focus.We also we had to buy the 12 steps of AA. Out of all this we learned about how much the body can take in when drinking. From men, and woman. There was a time looking back boozes become my demon. I paid my rent each mouth put food in the house, but I had to have my boozes over the week end. The after our dens loved seeing me. I never been homeless, but I have gotting so boozed up I would fall asleep were ever I was, one time I fall asleep wright next door to my house, in the street . and the den or the after hour joint I would buy boozes get drink fall asleep, when I woke up I Had not one cent in my pockets. All I can say is I did it again.

You can let boozes run your life, or you can bet it to the point by take hold of you life, as I have done. Your ego, what you many think,or do plays parts in your life. sometimes you many say this is not like me. The question comes to mine, do you know yourself? yes or no ! This comes back to you, and you alone.

I have looked back over my life, what have I done what have I missed. I Have seeing myself not caring for myself as I should have. What came to mine I missed my family, working all the time,making money was my gold in those days, having a good old time. Making friends, trying to fit in even thow it would hurt me in the long run .not caring for myself boozes was now part of my life.

Looking back from the age 20 to 35 years of age boozes was my down fall. I belived I was having a good old time, but I was doing nothing but killing myself.

Not remembering what I have done, or what I Have said to others, it could have hurt others,or myself. What comes out of ones mouth can and will hurt others.

Many times people would come up to me and said do you remember what you said to me,and my comment would be no! what have I said or do, man you was out of it, you was funny as hell, boozes would do that from time to time, I would get into fights, the next day I would have black eyes or cuts on my self Not knowing how I got them. Many people have blackout and don't know if they have them or not. Or how they got from point A to B You can a short term or long term blackouts. Between you and I My higher power looked after me, prayers, and those that cared about me, a seed was plated within me at a early age.it took root without me knowing it. That small steel voice within me, saying you know better than that, but I did not listen to it, I had to pay for my mistakes in life. Just as long as I listen to that still voice I'll be fine. You as a young man or woman must do the same. I needed to have a new birth .that new birth was not man, but it was GOD that did the work within me.I seening myself as a man that had no roof over his head, a man that has let man step in for all the wrong endives. Countless nights, crying myself asleep at night. Saiding to myself am not going to do that again but it took GOD"s mercies that took me from that point A to B. That night as the cops stopped me. Was a blessing for me.I could not have done it by myself. I needed help from others and I needed to help myself as well. One must come to grafts with one's self.

Church was my out let, I stopped drinking hinging out partying all night. calling myself having a good time. The joy I had within me was not by man, it was GOD the Father that worked from within worked it's way outward. And shined all over me. I had a new way of life. My hell was boozes nothing more. I got help but also I had to help myself. My family was glad I had changed my life, I had to prove myself to them, it was a hard to wake the walk ,I was round people that loved to drink. I had to walk away from the boozes and them. Some askd me man what's up with you, do you think you are better than us,I had to look them right in the eyes, and I said "no my life has changed I was killing myself by drinking I can't do it no more you need to do the same. you are killing yourself by drinking, "I had to stand up to them till this day am glad I did.

Most of my co-worker has died from drinking or drug over dose, God has away working thing out in your life. First I walked to work.

For three months I walk to and from work. Seeing my car parked man it hurt me to my heart. That I could not drive. I had no driver's license or car insurance. The day came, I got my driver's license and car insurance back. man that was a day of rejoicing, I did but not with boozes.I drove down to my mother's she laid me out for driving drink. "See that's what you get ,I told you not to drink and drive."

I will be in a risk pool for over 10 (ten) year's before I could get out from under it.

Now I don't drink any more, I stopped drinking now for about 40 fourty years now.

As for my sister man she's over joyed about me not drinking any more. there are times I fell like a drink, I see it but I walk away from it. Temptation is there but I will not let it get the best of me, no matter what.

The youth of today need to know about what's going inside there heads, when drinking and driving.if you ask them do you remember what you side or did, many will say no I don't, so many are killed by having black out's behind the wheel. Killing them selves Looking back that could have been me. take care an live.

POETRY

BY MARION ROBINSON

Open Your Eyes

Can you smile the roses that God has given us?

Can you tell a story of his dyeing love? Can you see the sun shining so brightly?

Can you see Gods Son in his Heavenly light?

Bitter Sweet

Lord teach me the way the things I need to know. At times am at fault, by the way that I squawk.

Can you help me in my daily walk?

The like of knowledge brings on a line of understanding. But the like of salvation bring on damnation.

Lord teach me the way to reciprocate my life.

Lord what goals have I in this life, that I can not see.

Is it that path of a wind fall, is it a waterfall that seems to seep me off my feet.

BaseBall

We play the game of baseball as a pass time. A sport that builds up the mine.

A sport that put a grim in one's eyes.

Think about another game of baseball in life marry go round. Where your life is at stake will you strike out

Will you hit a home run?

Will life give you a double play of an out?

Will life give you a run for your money? You may have men on all three bases with two out on account.

Will you hit that home run or will you make that final out. Yes it's a joyous sport.

But one game is forever, the baseball of life is what you make it. So stand tall

Keep your head up.

Keep your mine on the game. Keep it pure.

You can endure the pains of the storm of life.

Will You Get The Point?

I have no respect of persons, I come in contact with.

I have no color that will be my goal, my aim is to all that I may deceive.

I can waken you so your dreams will become your great nightmare.

I have torn families apart, if they are weak. But in other have become stronger and pulled together as a family should.

You thinkI ca't touch you. You are dead wrong, I can be around you for ten or more years, dormant am I.I can hit you all at once, often I do.

I'll make your life seems to have no meaning for living. I'LL even put you through pain.

Even death may seem to be the only goal. There's no such thing buying for time.

The only thing will be, how long will I have?

Make the best of your life, give that which is right to others. Bring the best out of you.

Repentance

As a body of Christ ,why can't the body come together as one body? are we so far apart that nothing we say or do will make a difference. We are to love one another, but can we?

As part of the body of Christ, why can't The body come together as one body?

Are we so far apart that nothing we say or do will make any difference?

We are to love one another but can we?

We take for granted the leadership that God has given us, that we are to follow giving such a hard way to go.

Doing our own thing, going our own way, from time to time forgetting what thing we are into or doing.

Most Christians are always complaining about one thing or the other. Or keeping things going, on that is not Christ like.

Are we in the world? If so we must come out the world and become Christ like,

can we? We become pure in our thinking can we become calmer in dealing with other.

Can we implant the love that is need for one another? We only pass this way only once

So why not make the best of it And be as a Christian should be.

Put away all the mass that seems to choke the life out of your follow man.

If You Cared !

There seem to be something wrong in our makeup of life.

How often one is put down, are we all not drinking from the same cup?

How can you embrace me when all the time you have a blade that is a piggy back in my back. cutting cutting cutting. Bleeding not of the pain of life, but bleeding from the hardship that I came across in life. Do you understand me? or do you really care?

Personally you say you say pitiful it must be to engrave with misgiving and not of praise.

Take a peek deep down inside, what do you see? What you see is very much real.

Don't ask me to conceal my most inner being. You try to read me, like you would a magazine going through page after page.

What would be your hypotheses?

Can you really say you have judged me, are you right by doing so? Be aware someone is witching you as well, calling the time and place an bittersweet Interject a respect for one another ,recollect all the good things that came along be in harmony, a jamboree of joy. Should be your goal a good seed you must be. Not an old weed which has nothing to only death if you let it.

Refection

We all have made mistakes in life ,but we don't let those mistakes stop us.

We learn by them, hopefully some do while others don't. Some are given a second chance

Hearing with ones ears is not a joke.

Seeing with ones eyes is not always on easy street. Speaking with one's mouth sometimes bring on disbelieved. Rolling up your sleeves with greate cheer.

Knowing some good work has been done. You can say yahoo yahoo when the day in done.

Bobby

The laughter that I share with you comes from within. The laughter helps me from cry deep down within.

Sleepless night, darkness less nights as countless demons creep in within.

Pain of discomfort, pains of life seems to hover over me. I shall not let this be. S shall I give up by no means.

Life I shall live pain let me be.

So my prayer dear God let me see another day .Help me to help someone along the way. Have thy own way, I shall hear thy voice I shall obey.

Existing

How can you see in the darkness without illuminated light?

Hidden lightless in it's somber sleep sleep sleep,sleep.how mystical is the darkness?

It makes you wonder of its dusky gloom, Adventurous takes on recklessness.

But yet complexion of many faces, has no prudent multicolor in the world of darkness.

Just a rush or ruin, that will bring on intimindation of the night Administer to the one that are crying out. Help me! Help me! Faceless people they maybe dishing out like corps like lifeless, yet moving can they be aroused .

thank about it!

Is There A Safe Place

Tell me how gentle maybe the times of life. Seeking a creed of life that may not succeed No matter how impotant it may be.

Sweep my weaker soul; to sleep Clef me within the very deep.

Bells rings with confidence. With its confidence

With its frankincense

So how blunt what you speak to me.

Do I give you acknowledgment or my comment just may imprison me.

The ills of pain is not my paradise conflicts within myself is the thief. So I besiege you with love and not with doom.

DeadBeats

Hello my name is terror ,and I have many friends that's with me. I'm with you each and every day. I make you're temperate to rise to the top of your head.

Like a bullet I fly so swiftly,

Speed would be my middle name. Then my friends fears stepping in.

He goes to the heart of the matter, you must think fast or he'll get you,

An alarm goes off inside of your head. Apprehension, faintheartedness, becomes a part of your anticipation of your presence danger.

Then come old doubt giving you skepticism, suspicion, and even disbelief.

Trust and weight out, what the outcome maybe. mistake can happen, have confidence in what you do.

Don't let three devastate you. You see they work hand in hand.

Door Bell

Someone is ringing my door bell. Who's behind my closed door?

Could it be keen or fold. Who is it I asked?

Who do you wish to see? The head of house

Well that will be me.

Give me a moment please, I'll be right there . Please take your time.

The gradual conversation that we had seemed very warm , though the door

This was not just any person standing at my door. A heart warm feeling came over me.

Something I never felt before, the voice seemed so sweet to my ears.

It seemed to over wham me.

As I open the door to seeing this man that stood it my door, Dressed in some old bag bond cloths to my dismay.

What do you won't I asked the man.

I have a gift for you this day,. This gift man can't give to you. Don't look at my clothes you may see there worn and tarred as it maybe.

Don't look at the man that stand before you that had nothing to eat. Don't look at the man that has no shoes on his feet.

Shire with me the joyous day ,tears was wiped away from your eyes. Don't turn me away this day ,you do know me .I was with you through deepest storms .

I was with you before before you were born.

I was there with you when you cried yourself to sleep.

Now will you let me into your heart today ,do you know who I am .

Let us break bread together and let me be your companion and friend.

Hope

How can you say there's no hope, for today for today has only begun?

The depth of seeing is not your hands. nor in mine .What hangs over us that make hope seem like a side show.

O how I hope to be a part of my life. With it coms that proclamation of being alive, living one day at a time.

Brother and sisters don't let your hope ,anddreams disappear, in the darkness of time. Stand tall and fight, take hold of life conservatory. Take that laxative that will clear your mine.

We stand side by side as administrators, in our own rights. Some rich, some poor ,some homeless, having no roof over their heads, some educated while other not so.

Each day I cry for you my brother and sisters, and I ask the question Why?

Where has hope gone.

What Is Your Will

Sickness has bonded up men's hearts

No longer can they see the light shining s brightly.

So many are asking why? Why me? Why me? Why me? Don't close the door too hope.

Truly darkness has hit us hard to the bone.

Some wake up with burden more then they could bare. Some cry out NO, NO not me !

Being afraid why my brother's and sister's.

Where's your hope? Tomorrow will be better than today.

Seeing the flowers growing, the green grass grow, Singing birds with a song and flying, you also have a song within your heart.

So look deep down within yourself, for that hope that is within you. Man can't give it to you, you must find it and you can .

The Cries Of A Nation

Mandatory is it why? What is happening to our people? Apart from seeing nothing but damnation that is put upon us. Druges, and all of it's demons runni9ng hear and their.

Putting a stop to life as know it to be .

Arefrigerator of cold hardness of killings, dragged down it's family me4mbers.

At time I can hear the brain waves waving , a slave to the dooms day, of the doorways of the heart. A spring leak running bloody down our streets.

The commonwealth of a nation so rich , yet so poor how can you let this be?

Is it crystal clear, what you have done, steering the gers of yesteryear that as brought us up four bearing the pains of today. How can you take a back seat ,are you not the architect of this conflict

You have barricaded yourself behind closed doors, not seeing not hearing, not even careing.

Awake you leaders of this nation of ours, The cries of a nation is calling you.

Where Do I Stand?

Why should I make an attitude adjustment?

There's nothing wrong with the one that I have. Why should I try to be Mr. Goody Goody.?

When people will to run over me!

Cold hearted seems to be the best way to go. Let nothing stand in the way

Let what ever comes come, I'll beat it down. Without a smile on my face.

But deep down within I don't wish to be this way. I need to let the sun shine in.

Being hard, cold, and broken hearted,

Will I ever stop being frustrated, with in myself.

Bring on the world and let me see what goodies that are within. Maybe oneday my life will change.

Maybe I will hear the songs that the robin sings. Maybe I will grow as tall as a oak tree.

Or maybe my heart will be change ,just as God intended it to be. A testimonial to others, sharing with others.